DP
DEMPSEY
PARR

Plants

Written by Martin Walters
Illustrated by Roger Kent and David Ashby

First published in Great Britain in 1998 by
Dempsey Parr
Queen Street House
4, Queen Street
Bath
BA1 1HE

ISBN: 1-84084-410-8

Printed in Italy

Produced by Miles Kelly Publishing Ltd
Unit 11
Bardfield Centre
Great Bardfield
Essex
CM7 4SL

Designer: Diane Clouting
Editor: Linda Sonntag
Artwork commissioning: Branka Surla
Project manager: Margaret Berrill
Editorial assistant: Lynne French
with additional help from Jenni Cozens and Pat Crisp

Contents

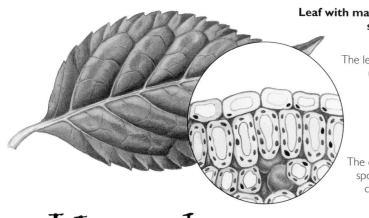

Leaf with magnified section

The leaf is made up of cells.

The dark green spots contain chlorophyll.

Why are most plants green?

Most plants are green because they contain the green pigment chlorophyll in their stems and leaves. Sometimes the green pigment is masked by other colors, such as red. This means that not all plants that contain chlorophyll look green.

How do green plants feed?

Green plants make their own food in a process called photosynthesis. Chlorophyll, the green pigment in plants, helps to trap energy from the Sun. Plants use this energy to convert water and carbon dioxide into sugars and starch. They get the water and carbon dioxide from the soil and the air.

How does a flower form so quickly?

WHEN A FLOWER OPENS OUT FROM A BUD, IT MAY APPEAR LIKE MAGIC in just a day or even a few hours. This is possible because the flower is already formed in miniature inside the bud, just waiting to open out. If you cut open a flower bud you will see that all the flower's parts are there inside the bud. The bud opens as its cells take in water and grow. Many flowers form their buds in the autumn, winter, or early spring, ready to open quickly in the warmer, sunnier weather of spring or early summer.

What does a plant need to grow?

Plants need water, mineral salts, and foods such as carbohydrates. Green plants make their own foods, while other plants may take in food from decaying plants or animals, or direct from other living plants.

The bud turns up toward the Sun and the petals open further.

The development of a poppy flower

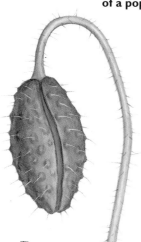

The bud begins to open in the warm sunshine.

The poppy flower is ready to burst from its bud.

How does a parasitic plant feed?

Parasitic plants do not need to make their own food, and many are not green. Instead, they grow into the tissues of another plant, called the host, and tap into its food and water transport system, taking all the nourishment they need from its sap.

Why do shoots grow upward?
Most shoots grow upward, toward the sunlight. The growing tip of the shoot can detect the direction of the light, and chemicals are released that make it grow more on the lower or darker side, thus turning the shoot upward.

Why do roots grow downward?
Roots grow downward because they can detect the pull of gravity. The root responds to gravity by releasing chemicals that cause more growth on the upper side, thus turning the root downward.

What makes a seed grow?
To grow, a seed needs moisture, warmth and air. Some seeds can only germinate (begin to grow) if they have first been in the low temperatures of winter. The seeds of some plants can lie dormant (inactive) for years before germinating.

The fruit capsule, containing the ripened seeds, is fully developed. The seeds can be shaken by the wind through the holes at the top.

The petals have fallen off, leaving the seed capsule.

How does a Venus fly-trap catch its prey?
The fly-trap is a carnivorous (meat-eating) plant that catches insects and other small animals. The trap is a flattened, hinged pad at the end of each leaf, fringed with bristles. When an insect lands on the pad and touches one of the sensitive hairs growing there, the trap is sprung and closes over the insect, and the bristles interlock to prevent its escape.

The poppy is now fully open with its petals unfurled.

How fast does sap flow through a tree?
In warm conditions, with a plentiful supply of water to the roots, and on a breezy day, sap may flow through a tree as fast as 40 in (100cm) every hour.

How do plants take in water?
Plants use their extensive root systems to take in water from the ground. Each root branches into a network of rootlets, which in turn bear root hairs. Water passes into the root across the cell walls of millions of tiny root hairs.

How much sugar does photosynthesis make in a year?

PLANTS TURN THE SUGAR THEY MAKE BY THE PROCESS OF PHOTOSYNTHESIS into other chemical compounds that they need for growth and development. They also use sugar to provide energy to run the reactions that take place in their cells. Some scientists have estimated that the total mass of green plants alive in the entire world make more than 150,000 million tons of sugar every year by their photosynthesis.

A strawberry plant

Strawberries reproduce vegetatively by sending out runners. The plantlet develops at the end of the runner and eventually grows into a separate plant.

Can plants reproduce without seeds?

Some plants, such as mosses, liverworts, and ferns, do not produce seeds. Instead, they spread by dispersing spores. But even among seeding plants reproduction without seeds is possible. Many plants can reproduce vegetatively by sending out runners or splitting off from bulbs, or swollen stems.

How are flowers pollinated?

POLLINATION IS AN IMPORTANT PART OF SEXUAL REPRODUCTION IN PLANTS. The pollen, containing the male sex cells, fertilizes the ovules, which are the female sex cells. This can happen in several different ways. The flowers of many trees release masses of tiny pollen grains into the air, and the breeze takes some to their destination. Many water plants produce pollen that floats downstream. Many flowers have evolved their structure, colours and scent to attract animals to pollinate them. The animal lands on the flower to feed from its nectar, gets showered with pollen, then moves off, transporting the pollen to the next flower it visits. Insects such as bees, wasps and butterflies often pollinate flowers in this way, but some (mainly tropical) flowers are pollinated by birds, bats, and even small mammals.

What happens in a flower after pollination?

After pollination, the pollen that has landed on the stigma of another flower of the same species will begin to germinate, if conditions are right. It sends a tube down into the style and eventually into the ovary of the flower, which it enters to fertilize an ovule.

How much pollen do flowers make?

Flowers can produce enormous quantities of pollen. Some American ragweeds can produce 1.5 billion pollen grains in an hour. Thus they can release 18 billion grains of pollen in one day. The American ragweed is a major cause of hay-fever, which is bad news for sufferers: US estimates put ragweed pollen production at a staggering 8 tons a week over a single square mile!

Why are many seeds poisonous?

Many mammals and birds eat seeds. Some plants have seeds that are poisonous to mammals and birds, which prevents them being eaten. Poisonous seeds are often brightly colored so the seed-eaters quickly learn to spot them and avoid them.

Which flowers are pollinated by mammals?

The flowers of the African baobab tree are pollinated by bushbabies and bats. Those of the saguaro, or giant cactus, in the southwestern USA and Mexico, are pollinated by birds in the day, and bats at night.

Why do flowers open in spring/summer?

In temperate regions many flowers open in spring or summer because this is the best time of year to attract insect pollinators. Ideally, the flowers open as early as possible in the season so that they can use the warm summer to grow and develop their seeds.

How many seeds can a plant produce?

In the tropical forests of Central and South America, a single trumpet tree produces 900,000 tiny seeds. These end up in the soil and germinate when there is a gap in the canopy (the roof of the forest).

Which plants have the smallest seeds?

Orchids produce the smallest seeds. They are microscopic and released in large numbers, to drift invisibly through the air. In some orchids, just 1 gram contains over 990 million seeds.

Where do seeds develop?
Each ovule is destined to become a seed, and develops inside the ovary of the flower. An ovule consists of the zygote, or fertilized egg, surrounded by the endosperm, the seed's initial food store.

How are seeds dispersed?

MANY SEEDS ARE DISPERSED BY ANIMALS. BIRDS EAT BERRIES AND PASS OUT THE tougher seeds unharmed in their droppings. Some fruit capsules have hooks that catch in animal fur and are transported that way, eventually falling free in another spot. Orchids have microscopic seeds that are dispersed by air currents. Some heavier seeds can also travel by air. The maple has "helicopter" wings, and dandelion seeds have feathery plumes. Many legumes have pods that split open as they ripen and dry, flinging out the seeds in the process.

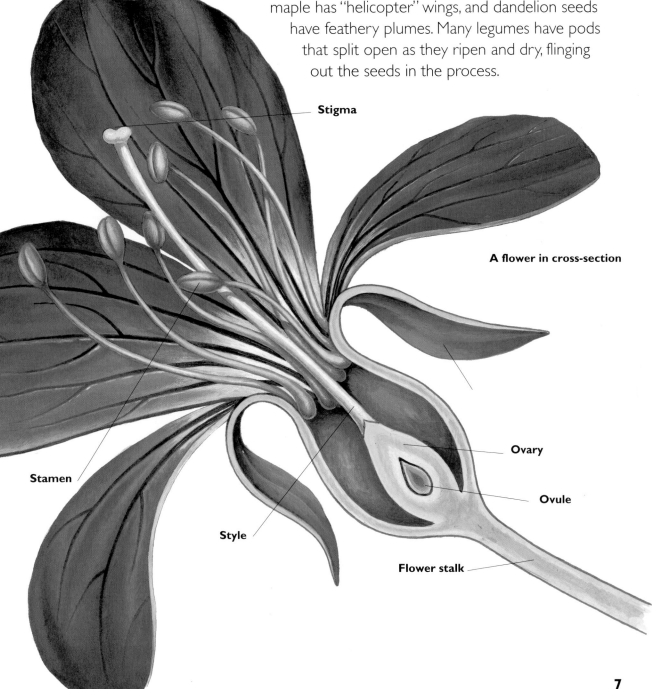

Stigma

A flower in cross-section

Ovary

Ovule

Stamen

Style

Flower stalk

How do forests help improve the air?

Forests help to preserve the quality of the air we breathe. They do this by releasing huge quantities of water vapor and oxygen into the atmosphere. Plants also absorb carbon dioxide, and help prevent this gas from building up to damaging levels.

How do plants colonize bare ground?

Some plants can quickly colonize bare soil. They do this by germinating rapidly from lightweight wind-blown seeds. Some colonizing plants spread by putting out shoots called runners, which split off, becoming new plants.

How do plants make the soil more fertile?

When plants die, they decompose, releasing the chemicals in their tissues into the surrounding soil. The mixture of rotting leaves and other plant material in the soil is called humus, and this makes the soil more fertile.

How are plants used to clean up sewage?

Sewage works use tiny algae and other microscopic organisms in their filter beds. The sewage beds contain layers of gravel and sand, which support the growth of millions of algae. These algae and other organisms feed on the pollutants in the water and help to make it clean.

What lives in a tree?

TREES PROVIDE HOMES FOR COUNTLESS ANIMALS, AND ALSO FOR OTHER PLANTS. The tree's leaves are eaten by the caterpillars of moths and butterflies and other insects, and many species of beetle lay their eggs in the tree's bark. Birds select a fork in a branch to build a nest, or use a natural hole in the trunk, and wild bees may also choose to nest inside a hollow tree. Many mammals are also tree dwellers, including squirrels, monkeys, sloths, bats, and koalas. In moist climates, other plants—especially mosses and ferns, and in the tropics orchids and bromeliads—can grow directly on the tree, in hollows where leaf litter gathers; they are known as epiphytes.

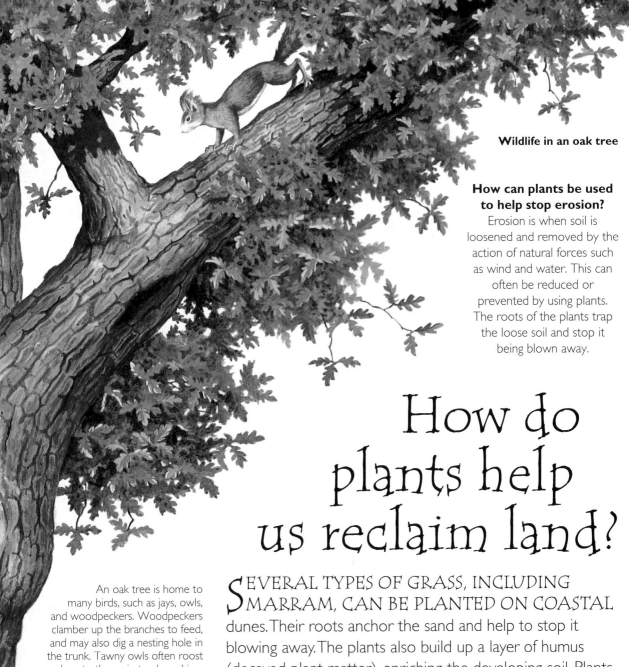

Wildlife in an oak tree

How can plants be used to help stop erosion?

Erosion is when soil is loosened and removed by the action of natural forces such as wind and water. This can often be reduced or prevented by using plants. The roots of the plants trap the loose soil and stop it being blown away.

How do plants help us reclaim land?

SEVERAL TYPES OF GRASS, INCLUDING MARRAM, CAN BE PLANTED ON COASTAL dunes. Their roots anchor the sand and help to stop it blowing away. The plants also build up a layer of humus (decayed plant matter), enriching the developing soil. Plants can even begin to reclaim land contaminated by industrial poisons. Some species have evolved forms that can tolerate toxic substances. They gradually improve the fertility and build up the soil so that other plants can grow there too.

An oak tree is home to many birds, such as jays, owls, and woodpeckers. Woodpeckers clamber up the branches to feed, and may also dig a nesting hole in the trunk. Tawny owls often roost close to the main trunk, and jays feed on the tree's acorns.

Many fungi, such as these bracket fungi, may grow from the tree's trunk.

How do plants recycle water?

Plants help to return water to the air through the process of transpiration. This is when water evaporates from the stems and leaves of plants. Water enters the plant through its roots. A column of water moves up through the plant, from the roots right through the trunk or stem, into the leaves.

What is the nitrogen cycle?

Bacteria in the soil use nitrogen from the air and turn it into a form that plants can use. Plants then use the nitrogen in their cells to make many complex compounds. When animals eat plants (or other animals that have eaten plants) they continue the cycle. The nitrogen returns to the soil in the droppings of animals or from the decaying bodies of plants and animals.

What happens to all the leaves that fall?

Huge quantities of leaves fall each season from forest trees, but they do not build up on the woodland floor from year to year. The dead leaves are attacked—for example by fungi and bacteria—and break down, gradually becoming part of the soil. The leaves are also eaten by many animals, including worms, insects, slugs, snails, millipedes, and woodlice.

Cacti are protected by sharp spines. Many kinds also produce large colorful flowers.

A cactus in flower

What are living stones?
Living stones are special desert plants from southern Africa. They have swollen leaves and grow low down among the sand and gravel of the desert surface, looking themselves very much like small pebbles or rocks. It is only when they flower that they reveal their true nature.

Which is the coldest desert?
Antarctica is sometimes called a cold desert, and is in fact extremely dry, because all its water is locked up as ice. The deserts of central Asia—in Mongolia and western China—are chilled in winter by cold air from the Arctic. Even in summer, when the days are hot, the temperature can drop at night to below freezing.

What is the strangest desert plant?
Welwitschia is probably the strangest desert plant of all. It lives for centuries, growing very slowly and producing just two twisted leathery leaves. It lives in the coastal deserts of Southwest Africa and gets its water mainly from sea fog.

Why are some deserts expanding?
Some deserts, such as the Sahara, are growing larger each year. This is partly because the climate is getting gradually warmer, but is mainly because the plant life on the edges of the desert has been destroyed by animals grazing there.

How deep do the roots of desert plants go?
Some desert plants have very long roots that can tap into deep underground water sources. Mesquite roots often grow as deep as 33 ft (10 meters), and there are reports of roots over 164 ft (50 meters) below the surface.

How do "resurrection" plants survive the drought?
When conditions get very dry, the leaves of resurrection plants shrivel up and turn brown. This cuts down the loss of water. When it rains, the leaves take in water, expand and turn green again.

What is a desert?

DESERTS MAKE UP ABOUT A THIRD OF THE LAND SURFACE OF THE WORLD.
They are found wherever there is not enough water available to support much plant growth. Examples of deserts are the Sahara, Namib, and Kalahari deserts in Africa; the Atacama in Chile; and the Sonoran in North America. Central Asia and Australia also have large deserts. Antarctica is also sometimes called a desert—although it is frozen, it is also very dry.

How big is the largest cactus?
The largest of all cacti is the giant cactus or saguaro, of the southwestern USA and Mexico. Saguaros can reach 66 ft (20 meters) tall, and 2 ft (60cm) thick. They can weigh as much as 12 tons and may live to be 200 years old.

How do desert flowers survive droughts?
Many desert flowers live for only a short time and set seed rapidly during the rainy season. They live on as seeds in the desert soil, until the next rains trigger the seeds to germinate.

Some deserts become a sheet of flowers after a rainfall.

What lives in a large cactus?

Cacti are home to a variety of wildlife. Their flowers are visited by butterflies and moths, and also by hummingbirds. Holes in cactus stems provide nest sites for desert rodents, and also for birds like the tiny elf owl.

What is a Joshua tree?

The Joshua tree grows in the Mojave Desert, California. It grows very slowly— only about 4 in (10 cm) a year—and its leaves can last for 20 years. The leaves have fibers inside, and they are sometimes used to make paper.

Which is the hottest desert?

Parts of the Sahara and the Mojave Desert in North America experience extremely high temperatures. The average summer temperature may be over 104°F (40°C). In Death Valley in the Mojave Desert, temperatures of 134°F (57°C) have been recorded.

What is an oasis?

An oasis is a place in the desert where water is in plentiful supply, such as at a pool permanently fed by a spring. Many plants can grow at an oasis, even in the heat of the desert. Date palms are commonly planted at oases, both for shade and to provide fruit.

How does a cactus survive in the desert?

CACTI ARE SPECIAL PLANTS THAT LIVE IN THE DESERTS of North and Central America. They have leafless, swollen stems that store water, and for this reason they are sometimes called succulents, as are similar fleshy plants of the African deserts. Since they lack leaves, they do not lose much water through transpiration. Most cacti are spiny, which probably protects them from being eaten by hungry (and thirsty) desert animals. Many cacti have furrowed stems. This allows them to expand with stored water after a rainstorm.

Which is the driest desert?

In parts of the Sahara the average yearly rainfall is less than 1 mm, making this one of the driest deserts. Parts of the Atacama Desert in Chile are also very dry – there, some years may pass before any rain falls.

American desert scene

The tallest plants in this American desert scene are the branched giant cacti or saguaros.

How do grassland fires start in nature?

Fires sometimes rage in grasslands, especially in the dry summer months. Fires can start quite naturally, for example when lightning strikes dead or dying grass. If a wind is blowing, the sparks can quickly turn into a fire that begins to spread.

Which garden flowers come from natural grasslands?

Flowers from the prairie grasslands of North America include the coneflower, sunflower, and blazing star. From the grasslands of Europe and Asia come flowers such as adonis, anemones, delphiniums, and scabious.

How do the plants survive fire?

Some grassland plants survive fires by persisting as thickened roots, and sprouting again after the fire has passed. Others may die, but germinate again later, from seeds left behind in the soil.

What makes grassland?

IN TEMPERATE REGIONS WITH WARM OR HOT SUMMERS AND COLD WINTERS, natural grassland develops in areas that don't have enough rainfall for trees and woods to grow. Many types of grasses dominate in these habitats. Mixed in with the grasses are other, mostly low-growing plants, many of which have bright colorful flowers to attract insects during the spring and summer. Grasslands have rich fertile soils built up gradually as generations of grasses and herbs grow up and die down, returning their goodness to the soil.

Why don't trees take over the grassland?

Trees cannot survive easily in natural grassland areas, mainly because the rainfall is too low to support their growth. But in areas where the rainfall is higher, trees will gradually invade grassland, unless they are chopped down or eaten by grazing animals.

What animals live in the grasslands of North America?

The original animals of the prairie were bison and deer, and smaller species such as ground squirrels and prairie dogs. The wild bison once numbered some 40 million, but was almost wiped out by settlers.

Where is the Steppe?

The Steppe—the grassland of Asia—cover a huge swathe of country from eastern Europe, through southern Russia, right across Asia, to Mongolia in the east.

A scene on the pampas of South America

Many parts of the pampas are dominated by tussock grasses, and very few trees break the monotony of the landscape.

What animals live in the grasslands of South America?

The animals of the pampas include such strange creatures as the mara (long-legged and harelike) and the plains viscacha (related to the chinchilla), as well as wild guinea pigs, giant anteaters, the maned wolf, and the rhea, a large, flightless bird.

Where is the pampas?

The pampas stretches across Argentina, Uruguay and southeastern Brazil, on the lowlands around the River Plate. The pampas is the largest area of temperate grassland in the southern hemisphere.

Where are the prairies?

The prairies extend from central southern Canada, through the mid-west of the USA, right down into northern Mexico, to the east of the Rocky Mountains. The area is known as the Great Plains, reflecting the open, largely treeless expanse of natural grassland.

What animals live in the grasslands of Asia?

Wild horses once grazed on the Asian steppe, along with antelopes and deer, but they are rare today. Many rodents live in the steppe, such as hamsters, voles, mice, and sousliks (a kind of ground squirrel).

What are grasslands used for?

Grasslands have long been used for grazing herds of domestic animals, especially cattle. But because the soils are so fertile, much of the original prairie land has now been ploughed up and planted with crops, such as wheat and corn.

Where are grasslands found?

THERE ARE GRASSLANDS IN THE CENTRAL PARTS OF ASIA, IN THE PLAINS OF NORTH America, and also in Argentina and in southern Africa. The Asian grasslands are called the Steppe and the North American grasslands are called the prairies. In Argentina they are called pampas, and in southern Africa veld. Smaller areas of natural grassland are also found in parts of New Zealand and in Australia. The steppes are the largest area, stretching from Hungary to Manchuria.

Cattle ranching is a common form of farming in many parts of the pampas.

Gentian

Many alpine plants, like this gentian, have large showy flowers.

Why is it colder in the mountains?

The Sun heats the ground and this heat is trapped close to the ground by the Earth's atmosphere. As you go up a mountain, and rise above the zone in which the heat is held, the atmosphere gets thinner and the air gets colder. It falls about 2°F for every 495 ft (150 meters) in height.

How do plants survive the cold?

Plants have evolved many different ways of surviving mountain conditions. Many grow close to the ground, in cushion-like shapes, which keeps them out of the wind. Some have thick, waxy, or hairy leaves to help insulate them.

How does the plant life change as you go up a mountain?

CONDITIONS GENERALLY GET HARSHER, THE HIGHER YOU GO UP A MOUNTAIN, and the plant life reflects this. So, there may be temperate woodland in the lowlands, but as you climb, this changes, typically to coniferous woodland, then to mountain scrub, then to grassland, then again, with increasing height, to a tundra-like vegetation, and to rocky screes and snow patches.

Why do different plants grow on different sides of a mountain?

Different sides of a mountain have different climates. On the south side (or north side in the southern hemisphere), there is more sun and conditions are warmer, while on the other side the snow and ice stay on the ground much longer.

How do mountain herbivores find their food?

Many mountain mammals burrow under the snow and continue to feed on mountain plants even at high altitudes. Others, such as marmots, store fat in their bodies and hibernate during the winter.

Why are alpine flowers so popular in gardens?

Many mountain plants, such as gentians and saxifrages, are known as alpines—because they come from the Alps. They are popular for their bright flowers, and also because they tend to grow well even in poor conditions, such as on a rock garden.

What is the timberline?

Trees cannot grow all the way up a mountain, and the highest level for them is known as the timberline. This varies according to the local climate of the region, but is around 9,250 ft (2,800 meters) in the Alps. Trees at this level grow slowly and are often stunted.

Alpine flowers

These alpine flowers are growing in a natural rock garden.

How do some mountain plants reproduce without flowers?

Many mountain plants have dispensed with flowers because of the lack of insects to pollinate them, and reproduce vegetatively instead. Thus some mountain grasses grow miniature plants where the flowers should be—these drop off and grow into new plants.

How can plants survive the snow and ice?

Few plants can survive being completely frozen, but many can thrive under the snow. Snow acts like a blanket to keep the freezing ice and wind at bay, and saves the plants from being killed. Alpine grasses stay alive and green under the snow, ready to grow again as soon as it melts.

How do mountain plants attract pollinators?

Many mountain plants have large, colorful flowers to attract the few insects that live there. Some, such as mountain avens, track the sun to warm their flowers, which attracts insects to sunbathe there.

What limits plant growth in the mountains?

THE CLIMATE CHANGES AS THE LAND RISES FROM VALLEY TO MOUNTAIN— it gets colder with increased height, and also windier. There is also usually much less level ground in the mountains, and the soils are thinner. Other factors that influence plant growth are the amount of sunshine, and the pattern of snow and ice accumulation. In very exposed sites, the wind chills the ground and prevents snow from gathering, creating conditions that defeat even the hardiest of plants.

Above the timberline in the mountains, many plants, such as edelweiss and mountain avens, grow well in the poor rocky soils.

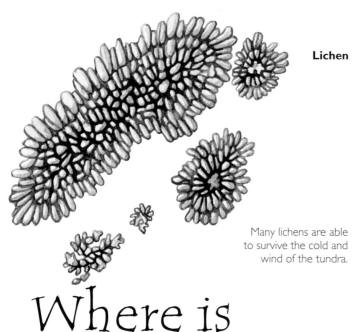

Lichen

Many lichens are able to survive the cold and wind of the tundra.

What is permafrost?
Even where the surface soil in the Arctic thaws in the summer, farther down it is permanently frozen. This icy layer is known as the permafrost. Because the ice prevents rainwater seeping further down, the surface can be wet.

Why are there so few plants in the Antarctic?
Most of Antarctica is covered with snow and ice all year. Only the Antarctic Peninsula has habitats where plants can survive, because it is warmed by the sea. Only two kinds of flowering plant—a hair-grass and a cushion plant—are native to Antarctica.

Why are there more plants in the Arctic?
The Arctic is surrounded by land masses—from Canada and Greenland to northern Europe and Siberia, with many islands. These offer many open habitats for plant growth, especially in the summer. About 900 species are native to the Arctic tundra.

Where is the tundra?

THE TUNDRA LIES NORTH OF THE CONIFEROUS FOREST BELT, IN A BAND roughly following the Arctic Circle. It covers a huge area of land—about 10 million square miles (25 million square km) from Alaska, through Canada, Greenland, Iceland, across to North Norway and Sweden, and on around the Arctic coast of Siberia. Only a small area of the Antarctic has similar conditions—the peninsula reaching north toward the tip of South America.

What plants do reindeer eat?
Reindeer (or caribou) survive the Arctic winter by foraging for food. They dig beneath the snow with their hooves and antlers to seek out tender lichens, mosses, sedges, and grasses.

Arctic scene

Why are many Arctic shrubs evergreen?

Many Arctic shrubs keep some or all of their leaves throughout the winter. Leaves formed in late summer stay on the plant, often protected by dead leaves formed earlier. Then as soon as the spring returns, the green leaves can begin to photosynthesize, so losing no time to make their food over the short summer months.

Why are many tundra flowers white or yellow?

Most tundra flowers are pollinated by insects. However, there are relatively few bees this far north, and the main pollinators are flies. Flies cannot distinguish colors as bees can, so the flowers do not need to be so colorful.

What is the tundra like?

THE MOST STRIKING FEATURE OF THE TUNDRA IS ITS TOTAL LACK OF TREES. Woody plants cannot survive here unless they are very small—there is simply not enough warmth in the summer for their growth. The dominant plants are grasses and sedges, mosses, and lichens, with shrubs such as heathers, and dwarf willows and birches. There are also many flowers such as saxifrages, avens, and Arctic poppies.

The plants of the Arctic include pretty flowers such as the Arctic poppy, low-growing cushion plants, and tiny trees such as dwarf birch and willow.

Why do many Arctic plants have swollen roots?

Many Arctic plants have swollen roots or underground stems. They contain food reserves in readiness for a quick spurt of growth in the following summer.

How do some polar plants melt the snow?

Several Arctic and mountain plants that survive under the snow have dark colored leaves and stems. When the Sun begins to shine, they absorb the heat and melt the snow around them.

What is the most northerly flower?

A species of poppy has been found growing farther north than any other flower—at 83°N, or on a level with the north of Greenland.

What is the temperate forest like in summer?

IN SUMMER THE TEMPERATE DECIDUOUS FORESTS ARE HUMMING WITH LIFE— birds and insects call from the trees, mice and voles rustle in the undergrowth, and plant growth is also at its height. The leaf canopy is fully developed, cutting out much of the sunlight from the forest floor. Nevertheless, most forests have well developed shrub and herb layers as well, with plants such as roses, honeysuckle, dogwoods, and hazel, and flowers including anemones, sorrel, and bluebells.

How are temperate forests harvested for wood?

Many temperate forests are not natural, but have been managed for centuries to provide a crop of timber. Traditional management involves a rotation of timber extraction, with only a proportion of the tree being removed at one time. This allows the forest to regenerate. Sometimes poles are cut from trees, and the trees can then resprout from the base, to provide another crop of poles later. This is called coppicing.

What else do we get from temperate forests?

Temperate forests provide us with a range of products as well as wood. Charcoal is made by slowly burning certain kinds of wood. In the past, people depended upon woodland animals such as wild boar and deer for food and skins. Many edible fungi, including chanterelle, cep, and truffles grow in temperate woods. Some woodland plants, such as brambles and wild strawberries, have edible fruits, and cherries and currants were originally woodland plants.

Why do most woodland flowers appear in spring?

By developing early they can benefit from the sunlight before it is shut out by the tree canopy. It is also possible that woodland insects find it easier to spot the flowers before the rest of the vegetation has grown up.

Which forest tree can be tracked down by its sound?

The leaves of the aspen tree move from side to side in the wind, and rustle against each other. Even the lightest breeze sets off their distinctive rustling, so the practiced ear can easily track down an aspen.

What lives on the forest floor?

The forest floor is a mishmash of dead leaves, twigs, fungi, and the roots and stems of woodland plants. The invertebrate life here is richly varied, with beetles, woodlice, worms, slugs, snails, springtails, ants, mites, and millipedes, to name but a few of the groups. These help break down the organic material, as well as providing food for small mammals such as mice and voles.

Why do the trees lose their leaves in autumn?

Trees and other plants that lose their leaves all at once each year are known as deciduous. The majority of broadleaved trees of the temperate woodlands are winter-deciduous, losing their leaves in the fall, and remaining bare through the winter. This way they shut down their main life processes, such as transpiration and photosynthesis, remaining largely dormant until the spring.

A year in a temperate forest

The trees in temperate woodlands lose their leaves in an annual cycle. Early flowers can benefit from the extra light filtering through in spring.

How old can forest trees get?

Many forest trees reach a great age, notably oaks, which have been dated at 400–500 years. Some woodland trees, like certain varieties of elm, which reproduce from suckers, are potentially immortal, as the original tree is constantly renewing itself, creating a whole grove of cloned individuals.

Which conifer is deciduous?

Larch is a coniferous tree—because it bears cones. But unlike most conifers, larch loses its leaves all at once, in the fall, so it is also deciduous, like many broadleaved trees. In fact, there are also broadleaved trees that are evergreen, such as the live oaks of the southern United States.

What is the temperate forest like in winter?

IN WINTER, THE TALL TREES FORMING THE WOODLAND CANOPY HAVE LOST ALL their leaves, the insects are quiet—they have either died or gone into hibernation—and there is not much bird song. Many of the loudest songbirds are summer visitors and have migrated south. Most of the flowers of the woodland floor have died back, many laying down underground stores of food for next spring's growth. Evergreen species such as holly, ivy, and yew stand out at this time of year, and provide valuable cover for birds and other animals.

A rain forest tree teems with life

Where are the rain forests?

THE WORLD'S LARGEST RAINFOREST IS AROUND BRAZIL'S AMAZON RIVER, and also along the foothills of the Andes Mountains. The world's main areas of tropical rain forest are in South and Central America, in West and Central Africa, in Southeast Asia, and in northern Queensland, Australia.

What are lianes?

Lianes, or lianas, are plants that clamber over and dangle down from the trees in the rain forest. They may grow very long and they use the trees as supports. Animals such as monkeys and squirrels use lianes to help them move about in the branches.

How much rain falls in the rain forest?

The tropical rainforests are warm and wet. In many, the rainfall is more than 80 in (2,000 mm) per year. It may rain at any time, but there are often storms in the afternoon.

How tall are the biggest rain forest trees?

The main canopy of the rain forest develops at around 95 ft (30 meters), with occasional taller trees (known as emergents) topping out at 165 ft (50 meters) or more.

Many of the taller trees have flanged or buttressed roots to give them extra stability.

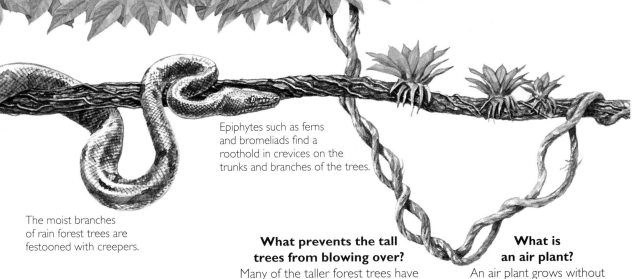

Epiphytes such as ferns and bromeliads find a roothold in crevices on the trunks and branches of the trees.

The moist branches of rain forest trees are festooned with creepers.

Which plants can trap their own rain water?
It rains very often in the tropical rain forest, and many plants trap the water before it reaches the ground. Bromeliads have special leaves that form a waterproof cup for this purpose.

Why are rain forests being cut down?
Many rainforests are destroyed so the land can be used for crops, or for grazing. Tropical forest soils are fertile, and many crops, such as cocoa and sugar cane, can be grown after the trees have been felled. However, the fertility of the soil is short-lived—see below.

How fast are the rain forests being destroyed?
Every year an area the size of Belgium is lost or badly damaged. Estimates in Brazil point to some 30,000 sq miles (80,000 sq km) of forest being lost each year, and similar destruction continues elsewhere. When the forest is cleared, the tropical rainstorms work directly on the soil, erosion sets in, and in a short time all the fertile topsoil is washed away, making the ground useless for crops.

What prevents the tall trees from blowing over?
Many of the taller forest trees have special supporting flanges near the base of their trunks, called stilts or buttresses. These make the tree less liable to be pushed over in a storm.

Why are the tropical rain forests so rich in species?
No one knows for certain, but it may be because they have been undisturbed for so long, and also perhaps because they have such a stable, warm climate.

What is an air plant?
An air plant grows without anchoring itself with roots. Air plants are common in some tropical forests. They get the moisture they need direct from the damp air.

What do we get from rain forests?
We get many things from rain forests, including timber, Brazil nuts, fruit, rubber, rattan (a kind of palm from which furniture is made), cosmetics, and even medicines.

How rich are the rain forests?

RAIN FORESTS ARE THE MOST COMPLEX OF THE WORLD'S NATURAL ECOSYSTEMS, with an enormous wealth of plant and animal species—they contain some 40 percent of the world's plants. They are the richest habitats on earth—for example, just 2.5 acres (1 hectare) of Malaysian tropical rain forest can contain as many as 180 different species of trees. The forests also contain untold riches in the shape of timber and fruits and herbs that can be used as food and medicine. The rain forests are important not just for their rich wildlife, but also because they help to preserve climate and soil stability. Without the tropical forests, climate change would almost certainly accelerate—the forests help preserve the atmosphere, releasing huge quantities of water vapor and oxygen, and absorbing carbon dioxide. If the forests are to be conserved, efforts must be made to use their resources wisely, without destroying the forests themselves.

How are wetlands damaged?

When soil is drained, or too much water is pumped from the land nearby, wetlands suffer as the water table is lowered. Wetlands are easily damaged by pollution as well. Sewage and chemicals released from factories easily find their way into streams and rivers, where they can upset the balance of nature and poison the wildlife.

Why do some lakes have very few plants?

Lakes vary in the chemical composition of the water that they contain. Some lakes, such as those draining from lime-rich soils, are very fertile and can support a lot of plants. Others, especially those whose water is acid (as in granite areas), are poor in nutrients and therefore poor in plant life.

How do water plants stay afloat?

SOME WATER PLANTS STAY AFLOAT BECAUSE THEIR TISSUES CONTAIN CHAMBERS OF AIR, making their stems and leaves buoyant. Others, such as water lilies, have flat, rounded leaves that sit boatlike on the water surface. They may also have waxy leaves, which repel the water and help to keep the leaves afloat, or upcurved rims to the leaves. Some combine wax with hairs so that the leaves are unwettable. Duckweeds are so small and light that the surface tension of the water is enough to keep them afloat, and the water hyacinth has inflated leafbases that act as floats.

Why is the water hyacinth sometimes a problem?

Water hyacinth is a floating plant with beautiful mauve flowers. However, it is also a fast-growing weed, and can spread rapidly to choke waterways, alter the ecology and impede boat traffic.

How does a lake turn into land?

Over time, a lake will gradually turn into dry land by a process called succession. Slowly, the remains of the plants growing in the shallows accumulate, making the water more and more shallow. Eventually, the edges of the lake dry out and land plants can establish themselves.

How does the bladderwort feed?

Bladderwort is a carnivorous plant found in boggy pools. The underwater stems develop small bladders, each with a trigger. When a small animal, such as a water flea, bumps into the trigger, the bladder springs open, sucking in the animal with the inrushing water.

How do river plants cope with the current?

FEW PLANTS CAN GROW IN THE CURRENT OF FAST RIVERS, EXCEPT for tiny algae encrusting stones on the riverbed. But in the eddies and slower currents of the river bank they can gain a roothold. River plants have to anchor themselves firmly with roots. They then tend to grow narrow ribbon- or strap-like leaves that offer little resistance to the water flow. Others, like water milfoil, have finely divided, feathery leaves, for the same reason. Water crowfoot sends up thin, flexible stems that bend and sway in the current.

Why do most water plants grow only in shallow water?
Most plants need to root themselves in the soil, even if they live mainly submerged in the water. In deep water there is not enough sunlight for plants to grow successfully.

How do water plants disperse their fruits?
The running water of streams and rivers carries floating fruits along, and there is usually some water movement even in ponds and lakes. Many floating fruits have tough coats that stop them from germinating too soon, so that they can travel a good distance.

What food plants come from wetlands?
The most important wetland crop is rice, which is grown in many parts of the world, notably India and China. Rice grows best in special flooded fields, called paddies. Another aquatic grass crop is Canadian wild rice, a traditional food of native Americans, and now a popular speciality.

How do water plants get their flowers pollinated?
Even though their growth is mainly below the surface, most water plants hold their flowers above the water, for pollination by the wind or by insects. Some, like the water starwort, have water-resistant floating pollen that drifts to the female flowers.

What is papyrus?
Papyrus is a tall sedge that grows along rivers and in swamps. It was used in ancient Egypt from about 3000 BC to make paper, but the plant is rare there today.

23

The fresh young leaves of the tea bush are gathered to make tea.

Tea leaves

Where were potatoes first grown?

Potatoes grow wild in the Andes Mountains of South America and were first gathered as food by the native people of that region. All the many varieties grown today derive from that wild source.

A selection of food plants

How is tea made?

Tea comes from the leaves of a species of camellia. This is planted on hillsides, especially in India and Sri Lanka, and in Indonesia, Japan, and China. The young leaf tips are harvested, dried and then crushed to make tea.

Which trees give us a sweet, sugary syrup?

The sugar maple has a sweet sap, which is harvested to make maple syrup. Most maple syrup comes from the province of Quebec, in Canada.

Which plants give us oil?

The seeds of many plants are rich in oil, which they store as a source of food and energy. We extract oil from several of these plants, including olive, sunflower, corn, soya bean, peanuts, oilseed rape, sesame, and African oil palm.

Which plants are used to make sugar?

The main source of sugar is the sweet stems of the sugar cane, a tall grass that grows in tropical countries. In some temperate areas, including Europe, there are large crops of sugarbeet. This plant stores sugar in its thickened roots. In some parts of the tropics, the sap of the sugar palm is made into sugar.

Sunflower seeds and olives are crushed to produce oil.

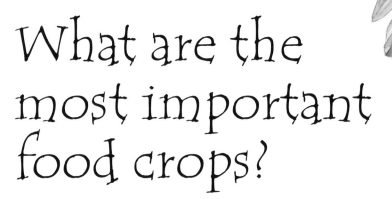

What are the most important food crops?

Millet and sorghum are staple crops in much of Africa. Rice is the main food crop in Asia.

SOME 12,000 SPECIES OF PLANT ARE KNOWN TO HAVE BEEN USED AS FOOD BY PEOPLE, and about 150 of these are in regular cultivation today. The most important crops are the cereals (grasslike crops)—wheat, rice and corn, followed by barley, sorghum, oats, millet, and rye. These form the basis of many people's diet throughout the world. Root crops are also widely grown. These include potatoes in temperate zones, and in tropical zones sweet potatoes, yams, and cassava or manioc. All these foods provide carbohydrates, while seeds of the pea family (known as pulses) are rich in protein. As well as peas and beans, these include soybeans, chickpeas, lentils, and peanuts.

Which fruits are grown for food?

FRUITS OF THE TEMPERATE REGIONS INCLUDE APPLES, PEARS, GRAPES, PLUMS, cherries, red and black currants, strawberries, raspberries, blackberries, and gooseberries. In warmer regions, a different selection is available, including citrus fruits such as oranges, grapefruits, lemons, and tangerines, and also pineapples, melons, dates, figs, bananas, coconuts, mangoes, papayas, and guavas. Some fruits have a more savory flavor, and are used as vegetables. Examples are tomatoes, avocados, and peppers. Fruits are very good for us. They contain energy-giving stores of natural sugar, as well as protein and vital vitamins. They also provide roughage to aid digestion.

How is chocolate made?

The cocoa tree comes originally from the eastern Andes in South America. The fruits, called pods, develop on the sides of the trunk, and each pod contains about 20 to 30 seeds—the cocoa "beans." The beans must be fermented, roasted and ground before they become cocoa powder, the raw material for making chocolate. Cocoa is now grown mainly in West Africa, and also in the Caribbean.

Where did wheat come from?

Wheat is one of the oldest known crops. It was probably first cultivated more than 6,000 years ago in Mesopotamia—present-day Iraq—between the rivers Tigris and Euphrates. Many useful crop plants have their origin in the Middle East. Other examples are barley, oats and rye, peas and lentils, onions, olives, figs, apples, and pears.

What is breadfruit?

Breadfruit is a tree, native to Polynesia, which grows to about 65 ft (20 meters), and has large edible fruits. The fruits are up to 1 ft (30 cm) across and are cooked before being eaten as a vegetable. The related jackfruit, from India and Malaysia, also has edible fruits, and these are even larger—up to 3 ft (90 cm) long and weighing as much as 66 lb (30 kg).

Wheat, corn, and barley are common in temperate regions.

Where does coffee come from?

The coffee plant is a large shrub, and its berries are used to make coffee. The ripe berries are harvested, then dried to remove the flesh from the hard stones inside. These are the coffee "beans", which are then treated further, often being roasted.

What is the Amazon cow-tree?

The Amazon cow- or milk-tree is a tropical fig. It takes its name from the fact that it produces a milklike sap, or latex, which can be drunk just like cow's milk.

Which countries use mainly herbal medicines?

IN MUCH OF THE WORLD, ESPECIALLY IN CHINA AND INDIA, HERBAL REMEDIES are used more than any other kind of medicine. Plants have been used as medicine for at least 100,000 years, and as long ago as 3000 BC, the Chinese had identified more than 350 medicinal plants. Today the Chinese use around 5,000 plant remedies; more than 8,000 medicinal plants are in use in India and Southeast Asia.

Which plant helps combat malaria?
Quinine, from the bark of the quinine tree, which grows in the South American Andes, can cure or prevent malaria. Before the widespread use of quinine, malaria used to kill two million people each year.

What plants aid the digestion?
Many plants, including the herbs and spices used in cooking, are used to help digestion. In Europe, the very bitter extract of wild gentians provides a good remedy for digestive problems. Plantain is another herb used for this purpose.

Periwinkle

What links willow trees with aspirin?
Willow twigs were once chewed to give pain relief, and a compound similar to the drug aspirin was once extracted from willow bark, and also from the herb meadowsweet. Meadowsweet used to be known as spiraea—hence the name aspirin.

Feverfew

Valuable medicinal plants

What is ginseng?
Ginseng is a plant related to ivy, and has been used in herbal medicine for centuries. It is claimed to help many conditions, including fatigue and depression, kidney disease, heart problems, and headaches.

Can plants help fight cancer?
Several plants are known to be effective against cancer tumors. One of the most famous is the rosy periwinkle. One of its chemical extracts, vincristine, is very effective against some types of leukemia, a cancer of the blood.

Which herb is traditionally used to treat headaches?
Feverfew is a pungent plant belonging to the daisy family. It takes its name from its long use as a remedy for fevers, and it has also been proven to be effective against headaches.

What links yams with birth control?
Wild yams provided the medicines for the first contraceptive pills. Both the female and male sex hormones can be prepared using extracts of yam, and the first birth-control pills were made using this natural plant extract.

Foxglove

Opium poppy

White willow

What medicine comes from deadly nightshade?
Deadly nightshade has bright juicy berries, which are also very poisonous. However, they can be used to prepare the chemical atropine, which is used to dilate the pupil of the eye in medical examinations.

Which plants help with breathing problems?
Lungwort is a herb with purple flowers and spotted leaves. It is used to treat asthma and catarrh. Ephedrine, from the ephedra or joint-pine plant, is used to treat asthma and hayfever.

What are coca and cola?
A world-famous fizzy drink originally contained extracts of two South American plants called coca and cola. The seeds of cola are chewed as a pick-me-up, because they contain caffeine. Coca is the source of the powerful anesthetic cocaine, which is used in dentistry. It is also a dangerous drug, if abused.

How can a deadly opium poppy save lives?

MANY USEFUL MEDICINAL PLANTS CAN ALSO YIELD DANGEROUS DRUGS, AND the beautiful pink-purple opium poppy is no exception. This poppy is a source of morphine—which is widely used as an anesthetic, and codeine—which is used in cough mixtures and many other medicines. However, addictive and dangerous substances are also made from the opium poppy, including the deadly drug heroin.

Which plants are used to make paper?

Most paper is made from trees, the wood being first turned into pulp. Some conifers are planted specially for making paper, but much natural forest is also destroyed for the paper industry. About 230 million tons of paper and board are produced worldwide each year. The main trees used are species of spruce and pine, as well as aspen, poplar, and eucalyptus. In India and Southeast Asia, bamboo is used to make paper. Straw and sugarcane are also used, as are reeds and other grasses, and also hemp.

What wood makes the best baseball bats?
The very best baseball bats are traditionally made from the hard and springy wood of the white ash. This type of wood has an attractive grain and is also popularly used to make cabinets and other fine furniture.

How many things can be made from bamboo?
Bamboo is one of the world's most useful natural plant products. As well as for making paper, bamboo is used for scaffolding, for building houses, furniture, pipes, and tubes, walking sticks, and (when split) for mats, hats, umbrellas, baskets, blinds, fans, and brushes. Some bamboos have young shoots that are edible.

How is cork produced?
Cork comes from a tree called the cork oak. This tree grows wild around the Mediterranean Sea, and has been cultivated in Portugal, Spain, and North Africa. The cork is actually the thick spongy bark of the cork oak. The cork is harvested carefully to avoid killing the tree—it is stripped away from the lower trunk, then left to grow back for about 10 years before the next harvest. Cork is used to make many things—from bottle corks, to pinboards and floor tiles.

What is kapok?
Kapok is similar to cotton and also comes from a plant, this time from a tree, the kapok or silk cotton tree, which grows in tropical America and Africa and can get as tall as 230 ft (70 meters). The fluffy seed fibers are used to stuff mattresses, jackets, quilts, and sleeping bags.

Can plants produce fuel to run cars?

WHEN TAPPED JUST LIKE A RUBBER TREE, THE COPAIBA TREE OF THE AMAZON rainforest yields an oil similar to diesel, at a rate of 4 gallons (18 liters) every 2 hours. This natural fuel can be used to run engines. The petroleum nut tree of Borneo and the Philippines produces a high-octane oil in its seeds, which is extracted by crushing. As the world's reserves of crude oil are used up, fuel from plants may become more important. Already cars run on sugarcane alcohol, especially in Brazil.

What is balsa?
Balsa is the world's lightest timber and floats high in water. Balsa trees grow in tropical America. Balsa wood is used for making models such as airplanes, and also for rafts, lifebelts, and insulation.

What is jojoba?
Jojoba is a low-growing bush found in the Sonoron Desert of Mexico and the southwestern USA. The fruits have a high-grade oily wax. It is used as a lubricant, in printing inks, and in body lotions and shampoo.

How many things can you spot in this picture that have been made from plant materials?

What is raffia?
Raffia is a natural fiber made from the young leaves of the raffia palm, which grows in tropical Africa. Raffia is used in handicrafts such as basketry.

California redwood sprig and cones

What is the tallest tree?

The California redwood, which grows along the North American Pacific coast, is the tallest tree in the world, reaching 365 ft (112 meters). Some Australian eucalyptus trees may grow just as tall.

What is the oldest plant?

The oldest known plant is probably the creosote bush of the Mojave Desert in California, USA. Some of these bushes are thought to be 11,700 years old. The bristlecone pine, which grows mainly in the southwestern USA, notably in the White Mountains of California, is also very long-lived. The oldest is about 4,600 years old.

What is the largest seed?

The coco de mer of the Seychelles has the largest seeds, each measuring 20 in (50 cm) long. They are produced inside a large woody fruit that takes six years to develop.

Which plant has the longest leaf?

The raphia palm of tropical Africa produces the longest known leaves. The stalk can be nearly 13 ft (4 meters) and the leaf-blade almost 60 ft (20 meters) long.

How deep are the deepest roots?

Roots of a South African fig were found to have penetrated 394 ft (120 meters) below the surface.

What plant can spread across the widest area?

THE BANYAN OF INDIA AND PAKISTAN OFTEN STARTS LIFE AS AN EPIPHYTE, a small plant growing on another tree. As it grows, it sends down woody roots that come to resemble tree trunks. Eventually it can cover a large area and seem like a grove of separate trees, growing close together. One 200-year-old banyan covered 493 sq yd (412 square meters), had 100 separate "trunks" and 1,775 proproots. The banyan is not the only tree with a peculiar spreading habit. The quaking aspen can spread from suckers and form a grove of trees that look separate, but which are connected underground. One aspen grove in the USA covered 106 acres (43 hectares), and was estimated to weigh 6,000 tons.

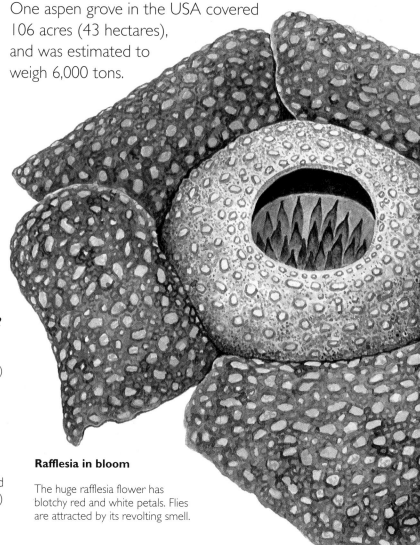

Rafflesia in bloom

The huge rafflesia flower has blotchy red and white petals. Flies are attracted by its revolting smell.

Which plant grows the fastest?

The giant bamboo of Myanmar (Burma) grows at up to 18 in (46 cm) a day, making it one of the fastest growing of all plants. However, another species from India, the spiny bamboo, holds the record for growth in a greenhouse—it achieved 36 in (91cm) in one day.

What is the world's longest seaweed?

Giant kelp is a huge seaweed that forms underwater forests in the coastal waters of California. Its fronds can reach 328 ft (100 meters), making it one of the tallest plants known.

What is the largest flower?

THE WORLD'S LARGEST FLOWER GROWS ON THE RAFFLESIA, A PLANT WITHOUT LEAVES THAT thrives in the tropical forests of Southeast Asia. It is a parasite, growing on the stems of lianes in the forest. Individual flowers can measure up to 3 ft (1 meter) across, making them the largest single flowers of any plant. Rafflesia's red and white flowers may look attractive, but they stink, mimicking the aroma of rotting flesh. The stench attracts flies, which then pollinate the flower. The largest flowerhead is that of a Bolivian plant, the puya. It is made up of more than 8,000 flowers and can measure 35 ft (10.7 meters) tall.

Which plant grows the slowest?

The record for the slowest growing plant probably goes to the dioon plant. The dioon grows in Mexico, and one specimen was recorded to have an average growth rate of 0.019 in (0.76 mm) per year.

Giant kelp

The base of the giant kelp is anchored firmly by its holdfast, but the fronds may grow up hundreds of feet through the water.

What is the smallest flowering plant?

A tiny tropical floating duckweed is the world's smallest flowering plant. Some species measure less than 0.012 in (0.5 mm) across, even when fully grown.

Which plant has the largest floating leaves?

The giant waterlily of the Amazon region has huge leaves. They grow up to 6.5 ft (2 meters) across, and can support the weight of a child.

Index